THE
BEAUTIFUL
BOOK

OF SONGWRITING PROMPTS

by Sarah Sheppard

For the songwriters with
songs still inside.

Contents

HOW TO USE THIS BOOK

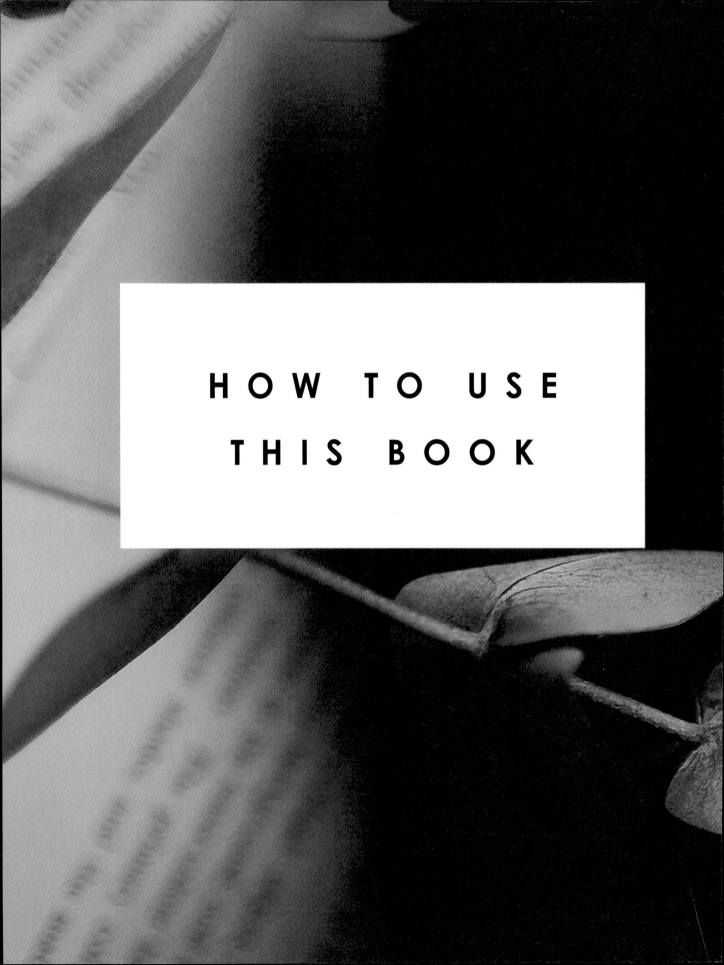

HOW TO USE THIS BOOK

HOW TO USE THIS BOOK

This book was created solely for your enjoyment. So that means, use it the way you enjoy it the most.

You came here to get ideas for songs. I hope these prompts are the starting points you need to let your creativity take flight. There are three types of prompts within: Word Sets, Settings, and Titles. There is also a bonus section at the end of the book that demonstrates other ways to remix these prompts and write new songs to them over and over again.

While there are no hard and fast rules on how to use this book, here are some suggest approaches you can consider.

These prompts are designed to challenge you. To get you thinking. To get your wheels turning and your pen scribbling. From there, it's up to you to pull out the song.

You got this. Write on, friends.

WORD SETS

Write a song featuring all 10 words in a set.
Or, write a song featuring 5 words. Or just 3.
Or, let the words spark something entirely different and just keep writing.

SETTINGS

Write a song to the prompt and answer the question directly.
Or, let the prompt fill you with more questions. Answer those.
Or, let just a single part of the prompt inspire something completely different and just keep writing.

TITLES

Write a song with the Title Prompt as your title and hook.
Or, write a song that uses some version of the title.
Or, let the title inspire another title altogether.
Or, start from the title then throw it away and just keep writing.

WORD SETS

Hidden
Rainbow
Cotton
Button
Sit
Differentz
Cake
Steam
Tripping
Earring

Almost
Vanity
Save
Flag
Gamble
Setting
Bicycle
Can
Attitude
Simple

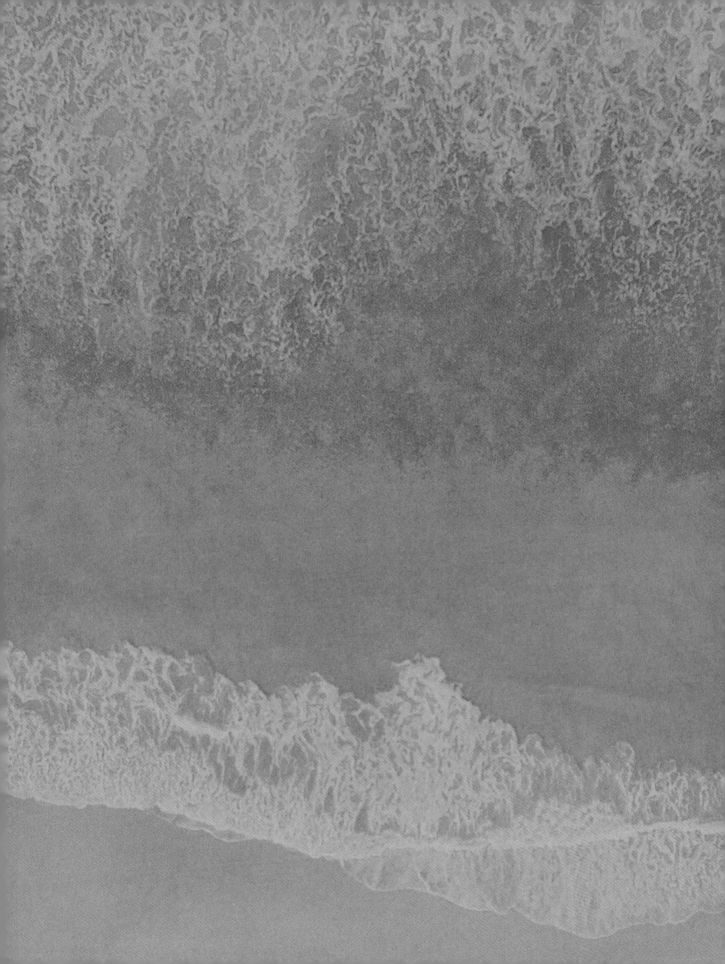

Timepiece
Radical
Daughter
Call
Two
Advocate
Letting
Major
Letter
Comfort

Amnesia
Fog
Prayer
Absolute
Join
Name
Sun
Diamond
Sinking
Minute

Tipping
Arizona
Knock
Finding
Appear
Tense
Rise
Saddle
Climb
Never

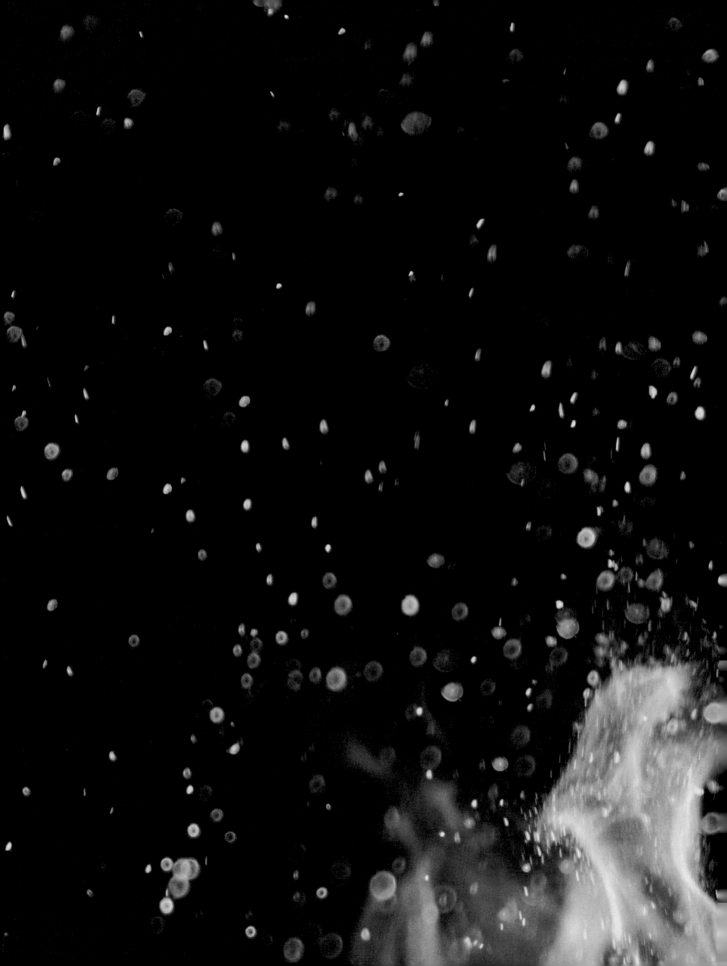

Raining
Accident
Triple
Minor
Bourbon
Ice Cream
Lake
Worry
Scatter
Spark

Willow
Crimson
Wander
Tide
Playing
October
Braiding
Feather
Lipstick
Anice

Seven
Fast
Easier
Single
Written
Letter
Torn
Awash
Rose
Bramble
Cover

Butter
Hills
Sugar
Board
Rise
Crinkle
Swept
Dried
Matters
Send

Swell
Set
Journey
Linen
Shade
Symphony
Won
Vacant
Alabaster
Worthy

Stop
Lean
Seychelle
Gourmet
Whitewash
Boards
Burlap
Full
Happy
Oak

Flicker
Play
Solitary
Rosemary
Muddle
Fine
Spirit
Sunrise
Family
Splash

Present
Cut
Same
Cocoa
Drip
Blossom
Tiers
Olive
Opal
Garland

Distant
Diamond
Vulture
Amaze
Silver
Help
Wind
Tower
Gleaming
Smile

Who
Title
Aside
Style
Glass
Bake
Shatter
Dare
Thunder
Accept

Cable
Save
Messy
Minute
Start
Final
Bowl
Fade
Kindle
Bone

Triple
Reach
Stalk
Tips
Outright
Familiar
Lost
Over-
grown
Today
Roam

Pristine
Ambient
Lemon
Flare
Shark
Twilight
Team
Underneath
Trip
Zero

Impossible
Porcelain
Engine
Fences
Pieces
Taped
Purple
Umbrella
Kissing
Aftermath

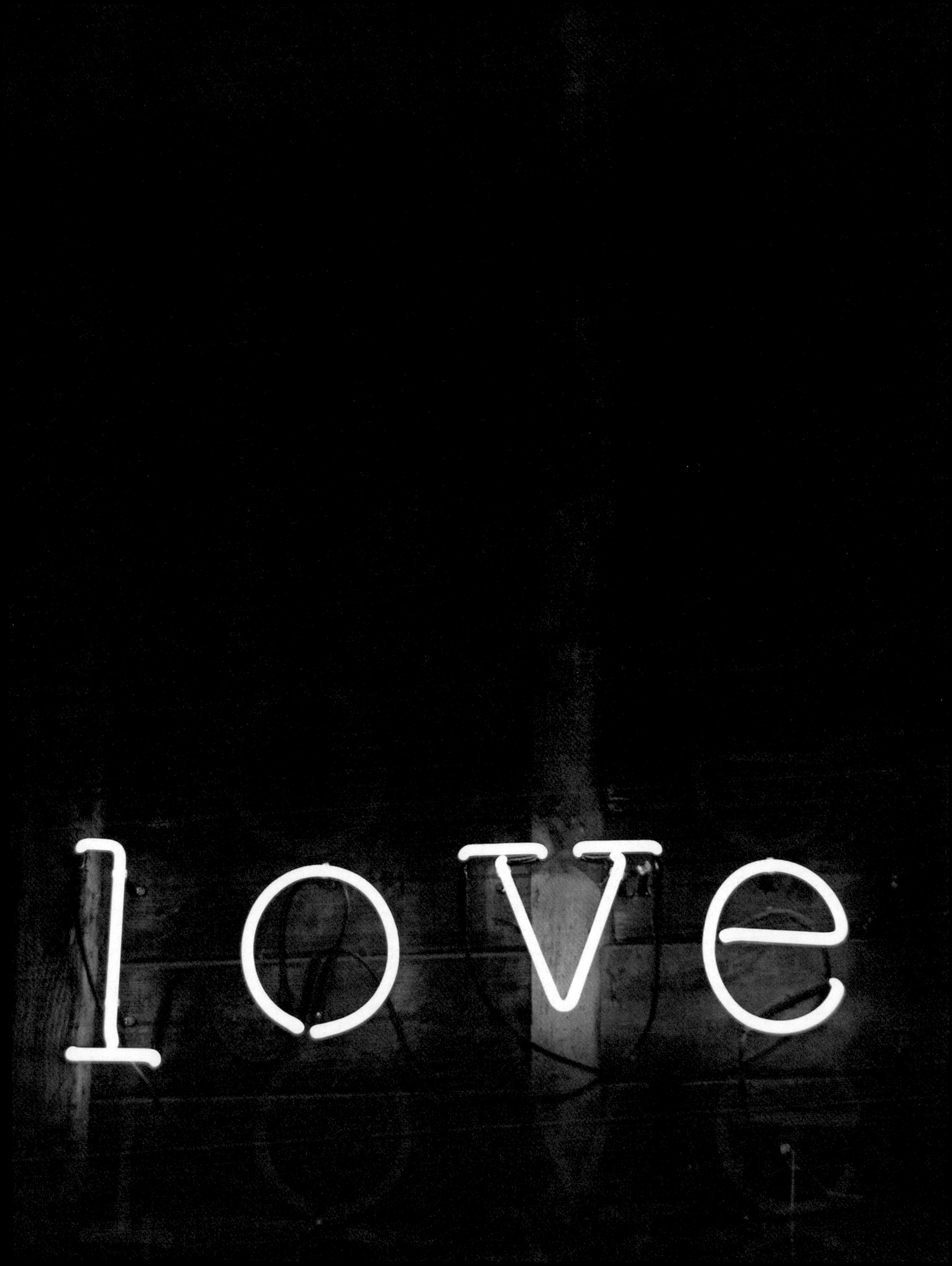
love

Missing
Pint
Awake
Hurricane
Ray
Brown
Drift
Daze
Keys
Ice

Wooden
Made
Mask
Skin
Between
Crumble
Distance
Alamo
Spotted
Cover

Absolute
Fresh
Learned
Difficult
Habit
Bookcase
Photograph
Return
Yellow
Covered

Scientist
Young
Order
Convene
Coat
Train
Away
Given
Running
Trade

Teeth
Lashes
Polish
Morning
Scrub
Passing
Lens
Tomorrow
Home
Tile

Endless
Daunting
Fog
Roller Coaster
Ignite
Persuit
Travel
Relentless
Take
Repeat

SETTINGS

1. It's raining on the boardwalk the entire week of spring break. What does everyone do instead?

2. She's scared to get on the tilt-o-whirl.

3. There was something in his tone of voice that you didn't trust, but you listened to him anyway.

4. He took off running, holding the kite string against the sherbet colored sky.

5. What is it supposed to look like at the end of the world, anyway?

6. Speedy checkout aisle shopping list: A bouquet of flowers, a book of stamps, as box of cigarettes, and an energy drink.

7. The cowboy coffee hit his system like a hard packed red clay brick to the cheek. It was time to ride.

8. How could I be the only person in the world who's watching this sunrise?

9. The fog wafting up from the mountains looked like ghosts. Where they warm?

10. Shine a flashlight in the dark and you have your own spotlight and your own stage.

11. The palm fronds pressed against the window, desperate for a break from the blistering delta heat.

12. If the light after a storm is the silver lining, what do you have to weather to get the golden thread?

13. Hold your head up high, pretty sunflower.

14. She painted and painted and painted every day until her story was told. Then she washed it all away.

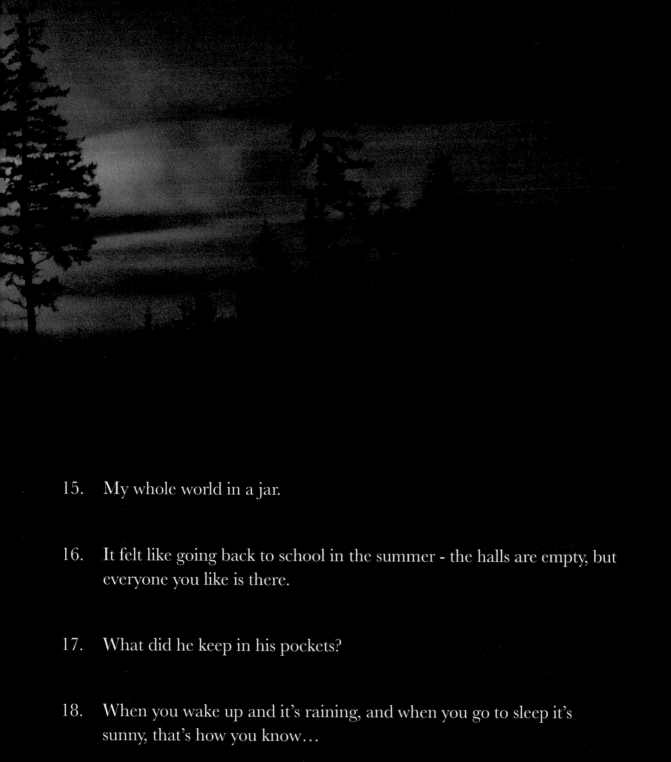

15. My whole world in a jar.

16. It felt like going back to school in the summer - the halls are empty, but everyone you like is there.

17. What did he keep in his pockets?

18. When you wake up and it's raining, and when you go to sleep it's sunny, that's how you know…

19.   White dresses on miles of racks, which one will have you and hold you intact?

20.   She wanted California, he wanted Louisiana.

21.   The light at the end of the tunnel, are you heading toward it or away from it?

22.   All the words you wished you'd said.

23.   I got here as fas as I could. Was it fast enough?

24.   Would you even recognize him if you saw him?

25.   I know what I missed out on. But tell me one more time.

TITLES

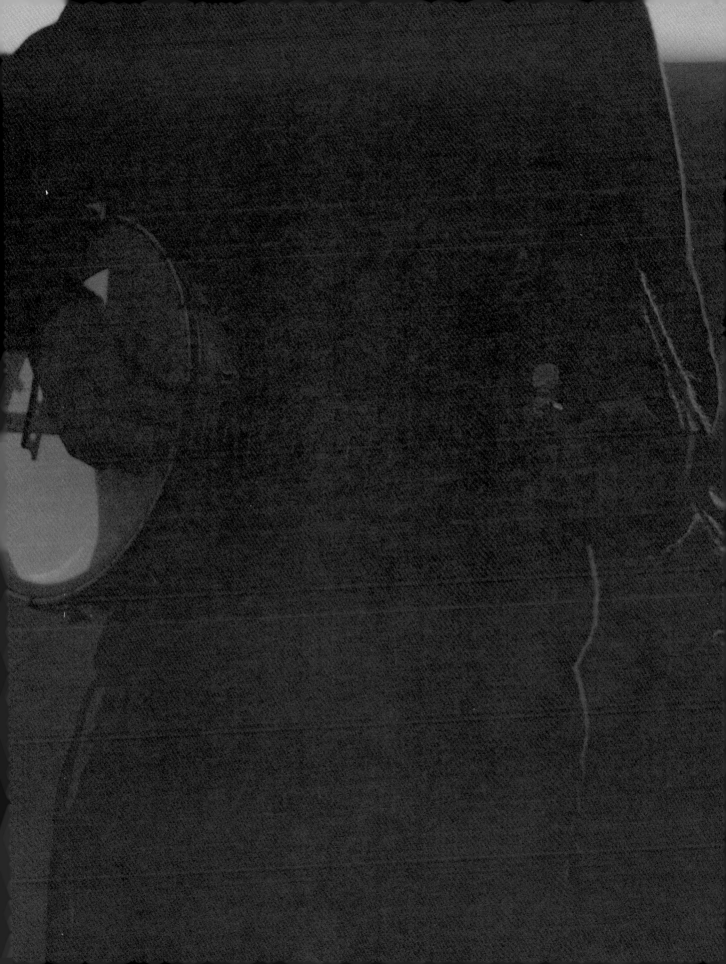

AGAIN

AGAIN: MORE WAYS TO USE THIS BOOK:

Flip to a random page. Grab a pair of dice. Roll them. Find the word that corresponds to the number you've just rolled. Pick another page. Roll again. Find the word. Repeat 2-10 times, or until you are fully inspired.

Every page has a photograph. A background story. Tell it. Who are the people in these photos? Where are they? What is happening just below the surface?

Use every single word from a Word Set in one song. All 10 of them. Make them make sense.

Mix and match Titles. What happens when you combine them? Do they become a new story?

Change the pronouns in the Settings prompts. How does the story seem to change with a different protagonist?

Make new titles from Title prompts by rhyming them. "Settle Into" becomes "Meddle in Blue." "Cabins and Castles" becomes "Sadness in Pastel." Let your mind wander to loose rhymes that are interesting.

Sarah Sheppard (or Sarah Spencer on stage) is a Nashville based singer/songwriter. Originally a Florida native, Spencer writes pop songs that have been steeped in the influence of folk, country, and popular music of the last 20 years.

Her songwriting has garnered many recognitions and awards, including winning the 2015 Frank Brown Song Contest and placing in the top 10 finalists in the 2013 NSAI Song Contest presented by CMT. Since then, her songs have been recorded and performed by other artists, and she's self-released an acoustic EP entitled "Freshman Year."

She's also the editor and main voice behind the contemporary songwriting blog, SongFancy.

Sarah lives in Nashville with her husband, where they write, cook, spend as much time outdoors as possible, and regularly travel back to the beaches of their home state of Florida.

16208897R20049

Made in the USA
Middletown, DE
23 November 2018